HAMISH AND THE SHADOW SECRET

Written by Liz Walker and Don Truss

Illustrated by Don Truss

Hamish and the Shadow Secret
published by Walker Inspirations
PO Box 1055
North Lakes, 4509
Queensland Australia
www.shadowsecret.info

First published in 2019

Text copyright © Liz Walker and Don Truss 2019
Illustration copyright © Don Truss 2019

Written by Liz Walker and Don Truss
Illustrations by Don Truss
Design by Jane Maughan, Creative Peek
Editing by Ali Stegert

This publication (which includes guidance notes) is designed to provide helpful information to our readers relating to prevention of pornography harms. This book is not intended as a substitute for the advice or services of mental health or other professionals. Content is provided in good faith to improve online child protection measures and to raise awareness. Readers and their carers are responsible for their own choices, actions, and results.

The publisher and the individual authors disclaim responsibility for any adverse consequences which may occur directly or indirectly as a result of using or applying any contents within this publication.

All rights reserved. No part of this publication may be reproduced, stored in a retrieval system, or transmitted in any way or by any means, electronic, mechanical, photocopying, recording or otherwise, without the prior written permission of Walker Inspirations.

Printed through KDP and IngramSpark.

Cataloguing-in-Publication Data

Creators:	Walker, Liz, author
	Truss, Don, author
Title:	Hamish and the Shadow Secret
ISBN:	978-0-9580279-6-0
National Library of Australia Cataloguing-in-Publication entry:	NLApp85689
Target Audience:	Children aged 8–12-years-old
Subjects:	Online Safety
	Protective Behaviours
	Autonomy in children
	Juvenile literature
Other Authors/Contributors:	Truss, Don, illustrator

Dedication

From Liz: To my three inspiring kids who have learnt how to be strong, respectful and brave! My full mama-heart is so proud of you all! One day, you may have families of your own and they too, will make powerful choices!

From Don: To my four wonderful children and the many kids I have journeyed with as a chaplain. With the hope that you will know the precious treasure that is your heart and the great value in guarding it. You are worth it.

TABLE OF CONTENTS

A Day I Will Never Forget 1
The City of the Guardians 7
The Mystery 11
Following the Map 15
The Device 19
The Battle Inside Me 27
The Shadow Secret 29
The Gentle Hero 35
The Power of Choice 41
Secrets Revealed 45
Getting Stronger 49
Training to be a Guardian 51
3 Steps to Being Safe 60
Note to Parents, Carers and Teachers 62
About the Author 64
About the Illustrator 65

CHAPTER 1

A DAY I WILL NEVER FORGET

At nine years old, I should have known better than to talk to strangers. But that's exactly what I did. Wow, was that a big mistake!

"Psst. Oi!"

I was taking the shortcut home—it's pretty safe where I live. The City of The Guardians is surrounded by ancient wrap-around towering walls. Pockets jingling with money I'd earned doing chores, I was imagining fun ways to spend my earnings when I heard a weird hissing sound.

"Psst!"

An older kid I'd never seen before was standing in the shadows, which, when you think about it, is kind of creepy. His hoodie draped over his head and almost completely covered his face which was even creepier.

"Who? Me?" I asked.

He nodded and beckoned me over.

Just ignore him Hamish. "Keep walking," my thoughts warned me. Silly me—I didn't listen to the voice in my head. Instead I went straight over to him. My tummy tightened like a fist. Whoa—that felt yucky. I wonder why...

This kid, who I immediately nicknamed "Shadow Boy", reached out and gave me a small piece of paper. "Take this and **don't show anyone,**" he said. "You'll need it later."

"What is it? What do I need it for?"

"You'll need it when you find the **tech device,**" whispered Shadow Boy. "It's kept deep within the city walls and it's something that The Guardians go to great lengths to hide from us".

"Why do they hide the device from us?"

Shadow Boy snickered. "Beats me. I reckon everyone should check it out."

I cautiously opened the folded piece of paper, half expecting something to jump out at me. All I could see were some jumbled letters.

Shadow Boy smirked. "It's a code to help you unlock the tech device. When you type in this password, you'll be able to search for anything in the world!"

"Wow! Anything?" This thing must be powerful.

"Oh yeah," he said with a sneer. "You will be able to see and hear things you could never imagine." He rambled on about buttons and bright screens, but I didn't really take in what he was saying. I was too distracted by the weird sensation in my gut—like something was wrong.

"But don't let anyone see you! It's our little secret."

CHAPTER 2

THE CITY OF THE GUARDIANS

Nothing like this had ever happened to me before. I guess it's because I live in *The City of The Guardians*. Many years ago, the fortress walls kept our ancestors battle-ready and safe from intruders. We are still one of the most protected cities around—shady characters like Shadow Boy aren't common in these parts.

Dad is an honest and hard worker in the market place, Mum is a Guardian, and I go to the local school with my two sisters and my best friends—Jasmine, Blade, Caleb and Rose.

Guardians are awesome—all my friends think so too! They keep watch over our great city, shielding us from things that could harm.

Admired by everyone, The Guardians train every day. They lead by example and are **strong** yet **gentle**. They are **respectful, courageous** and **brave**, and are known to be **wise**. It took me a while to work out what a wise person is, but Mum says it's someone who learns from their mistakes, respects others and thinks carefully about their choices.

My favourite part about living here is hanging out with my friends after school at training. We learn how to handle the basic tools of The Guardians and practice the values that make them so famous and respected.

I would love to be chosen as a Guardian one day, just like my mum. She gets to keep families safe, protect the city and pass on her skills to me and my friends. The lead Guardians choose only the best to join them—I have no idea if I'll ever be good enough!

The City of The Guardians is rich with history and values, but not everyone likes it so much. I've heard people complain that we are stuck in a time-warp—some sort of old-fashioned fuddy-duddies. Rumours say that other places in the world have way more technologies than our city. I've often wondered what it would be like to use exciting tech devices... and now, because of Shadow Boy, maybe I can finally find out!

CHAPTER 3

THE MYSTERY

Ugh...What do I do??

The tightness in my tummy got worse around Dad. If I told Dad about Shadow Boy and the slip of paper, it would probably feel better... but really, what could be so bad about a string of letters? The Guardians use it, so it couldn't be so bad... but then why did Shadow Boy tell me I can't show anyone?

I decided to keep it a **secret** and hide the little piece of paper. I was a Keeper of Secrets. Surely Shadow Boy didn't pick just anyone. Out of all the kids, he picked me!

So, what was this mysterious tech device anyway? On second look, I noticed that there was a map on the back of the piece of paper. I know that place. It's where The Guardians work in the heart of the city.

Why me? Why this? What if? All kinds of questions and wonders whizzed around inside my head. My tummy tingled and burned with every what-if.

I knew I should speak to someone, but who? Jasmine? What if she told me not to? Dad? What if Dad said no? Then I would never know what it was!

I couldn't shake the fact that something about this felt wrong, but I also felt special that Shadow Boy chose me out of everyone. And Shadow Boy told me **I should not show anyone...**

But could I trust him...? I trust my dad... Shadow Boy was a stranger...

I wrestled all night with my thoughts, wondering what I should do. While my family were still asleep and before the sun rose, I crept out of my house.

I'd never stop thinking about this—I had to find out! Then I could move on and forget about it.

What would the words on the paper unlock? What would I see?

But wait... why would Shadow Boy know about something that was kept hidden from the rest of us?

These questions and many more kept drumming loudly in my head.

CHAPTER 4

FOLLOWING THE MAP

I made my way through the streets until I came to the place marked on the map right near the markets. I usually love coming here to see Dad—he always gives me a piece of fruit from his stall. There's no way I could eat anything now—I could barely swallow!

I had joked with Jasmine, Blade, Caleb, and Rose about the gap in the wall at the markets being like a portal that might take us into some sort of hidden world. Maybe we were right—the sooner I worked out the mysterious code on the other side of this wall, the better!

I scanned the path behind me. What if someone I knew saw me? Mum's Guardian friends or a neighbour? I swallowed the lump in my throat. "Just go!" I told myself. I crawled through the gap in the wall that led me to a winding passage.

With each step down the passage, my heart pounded faster. I walked past heaps of rooms, but none of them seemed "special" enough to hold something as exciting as the tech device. That was until I reached a door with a big handle that had the seal of The Guardians etched upon it. The sign said, "Guardians Only". This had to be it!

CHAPTER 5

THE DEVICE

I pushed on the door and for the first time, noticed my palms were sweaty. Oh boy, I was freaking out on the inside!!

Something glowed in the corner. Was that the tech device? It had a screen and a board covered with buttons— Shadow Boy's ramblings seemed to make sense now.

I quickly pulled out the folded piece of paper and opened it up. I could see that the symbols of the code matched the buttons on the keyboard.

My heart was thumping out of my chest as I sat in the chair. What is going on with my body? Is it excitement? Curiosity? Whatever it was, I was burning up!

My inner voice screamed, "Oh man... What are you doing!? Should you even be here? A Guardian could walk in at any moment... What are you gonna do then?!"

The code was in big, bold writing. My fingers trembled as I typed but I had come too far to turn back now.

I found the keys on the board that matched the code...

And...

Then...

Wow!!!

I found all kinds of things. This was amazing. There was so much I could see and explore!

I'd been on all kinds of adventures with Jasmine, Blade, Caleb and Rose but nothing like this. Shadow Boy was right! I could see and hear things I had never thought imaginable!

Wonderous pictures of far-away places in the world, exciting things to learn, story-type pictures that moved and lots of places to click—a never-ending adventure unfolded on this glowing screen!

But just then, out of nowhere, an image of naked people popped up on the screen. Ahh! What—why? Yikes! My neck and cheeks burned. I pecked wildly at keys, trying to delete the image.

My tummy felt like it does when Dad makes us eat his "special" stew that I hate. Grossed out!

Eeek! Another image popped up! While my brain was telling me one thing, my body wanted me to keep looking and I found it really hard to stop.

Argh! My body played tricks and reacted in crazy ways. My private parts felt warm, tingly and excited—I was curious and wanted to see more but my head was screaming at me to look away. Something had woken up inside me.

No one had EVER said anything to me about this! Is this what Shadow Boy was talking about? Is this why he told me not to show anyone the code? Is this wrong?

Inside me, a battle roared. I was being pulled in two different directions. The images on the screen fought with the values that The Guardians had taught me.

Surely it wouldn't hurt to look a little more. Besides, no one would ever know...

I must have lost track of time—footsteps in the passage snapped me back to reality. The steps seemed to stop in the next room. Quickly, I closed everything down and snuck out the way I'd come in.

What had just happened? I thought about it over and over as I made my way home. I wanted to crawl back under the covers of my bed—my head still racing with the things I had seen.

CHAPTER 6

THE BATTLE INSIDE ME

What had I done? A voice inside me told me it wasn't right. But the battle raged, and something had awoken—a desire to see more.

I wanted to look again, but at the same time, I never wanted to look again. What was this? Why was there a tug of war going on?

I tried to be strong and act normal but this secret was sucking the life out of me.

The next day at school I pretended everything was okay but I found it so

hard to concentrate. I was distracted during Guardian training.

"Are you okay—something seems off?" asked Jasmine, my closest friend.

Did she know? I brushed her off. "I'm just tired. I didn't sleep well last night." I had to keep this from everyone—NO ONE could know. Nobody could possibly understand. I was stuck.

As the week went by, I snuck out to look at the device a few more times. I felt so guilty, but the more I looked, the more I wanted to go back and see where these searches would lead.

It didn't feel as "dirty" as the first time, and it always felt like there was **something pulling** me, **drawing me** back to see more. But something else pulled me another way.

CHAPTER 7

THE SHADOW SECRET

Every time, I snuck out just before dawn, following the same path to the gap in the wall and down the winding passage. I sat in the chair and opened the device up again. I experienced the same crazy feelings and reactions as every other time. I was being swallowed up by some sort of invisible spinning force. I couldn't break free.

One time, I spotted a flashing link I had not seen before. When I pressed the key, it opened the screen to things that turned my stomach over. Violent and hurtful things that almost made me throw up.

I had to STOP. I quickly wiped the screen blank and shut it down. BUT... **I couldn't delete the pictures from my mind!** I couldn't close them down!

I must be sick to want to see this! Why am I so weak that I can't stop myself? It's wrong, so there must be something wrong with me too! I can't trust myself.

But I couldn't help wondering what else I would find... my body was tricking me.

Do people actually do this stuff? Was this real? My parents had spoken a little about what happens as boys and girls grow up and where families come from. They taught me about love and showed me what it means to respect others, but this seemed to be the exact opposite.

Once again, I snuck through the shadows to my home, where everything was normal and good—everything but me. I was lying, sneaking, and full of sickening thoughts. What had happened to my simple life?

That week, I couldn't focus on anything. I'd fallen behind in my Guardian training. It seemed like there was a massive wall of silence between my dad and me. Mum must have sensed something wasn't right. She pestered me with questions. My sisters' normal silliness annoyed me—everything annoyed me. When I snapped at Chloe, her eyes filled with tears. **"What's wrong with you?"**

My thoughts haunted me. I couldn't stop them, couldn't control them... They started changing. They were dirty—even about my friends. At school, Jasmine spoke words that left me feeling hollow.

"What's happened to you? You've CHANGED!!"

She was right. I had changed. I was changing more.

I couldn't think straight. I lost my appetite and wasn't sleeping well. Sometimes I had nightmares, reliving the images in the dark hours of the night. Anger and confusion followed me everywhere like a cloud.

I couldn't even talk because the thoughts were too loud. I was left with more questions than when I first held that little piece of paper in my hands.

I wish I had never met Shadow Boy! I wish I had just thrown the paper away at the start!

It was too late to change any of that, but I had to do something. I needed to get help. These crazy thoughts were getting worse, and the ones I loved the most could see that something was wrong.

I just had to speak to someone I could trust. But who?

CHAPTER 8

THE GENTLE HERO

I thought long and hard and remembered an old, trusted family friend who was known for giving wise advice. They had once been a Guardian and were now known throughout the city as a Gentle Hero. I had always felt safe around them. Maybe they could help me... it couldn't hurt. It can't be worse than this!

The Gentle Hero lived in the fields outside the hustle and bustle of the city—our family had visited many times. As I walked to the Gentle Hero's

home, I looked back to the huge city walls... the walls that were meant to protect us. I couldn't help but think... those walls couldn't protect me from what I saw.

If those walls could not protect me from these images or thoughts, then what could?

When I finally arrived, the Gentle Hero was in the field. As they saw me approaching, they put down their tools and were immediately ready to listen. Seeing this reminded me that hard work and helping others were part of The Guardian values.

We sat down under an Oak tree at the side of the field. It was so clear and beautiful—the air was fresh.

"Hamish, you look like you're carrying a huge weight. Is there anything I can do?"

Those few gentle words were the key to unlocking the Shadow Secret I had been holding. I began to pour out the deep things that had consumed me for these past few weeks. With my head down, I shared everything. I spoke about where this dark journey had begun with Shadow Boy, and how I kept wanting to go back to the device—even though a part of me didn't.

"I feel like there are two people wrestling inside myself, but one is stronger. I just can't make sense of any of it."

The Gentle Hero listened intently to what I was saying and instead of telling me I was some sort of weirdo, they nodded and seemed to understand.

Once I had finished sharing all that was on my heart, the weight and confusion lifted and the fogginess in my head began to clear. It felt as though the Shadow Secret was losing its hold.

CHAPTER 9

THE POWER OF CHOICE

This Gentle Hero helped make sense of what was happening to me. "You see Hamish, when we see, hear or experience things that trouble or confuse us, it's very important to talk with a trusted person."

Speaking with the Gentle Hero didn't take away what I had seen but it helped to know that someone I trusted understood and wanted to help me through this.

"I feel so much better knowing that it's normal for me to feel confused about this". The Gentle Hero was right—sharing this Shadow Secret helped me feel less anxious and more peaceful.

I learnt a lot about my 'self'.

The Gentle Hero explained, "Hamish, our 'self' is a bit like The City of The Guardians. We all have lots of different parts—our mind, body, emotions, and relationships."

"Just like the walls protect our city, you also need to guard the things that go into your mind, be aware of the ways your body changes, keep watch over how your emotions feel, and practice self-control."

The Gentle Hero said that by practising these things, I would build wise character.

"So, you mean that just like I've been training in the hopes of becoming a chosen Guardian, I also need to learn to skilfully guard my 'self'?"

"Exactly!" my hero friend agreed. "You are responsible for protecting the wonder that comes with life, being you, and growing up. And it's **up to you** to battle against the things that may seek to harm you and steal and control your thoughts."

I learnt that this process takes time and that sometimes we make mistakes. But every Guardian needs to learn to guard their own 'self' before they can guard the city.

I now realise that I have a choice. I could choose to go back to what Shadow Boy showed me, or I could choose not to.

It gave me so much courage to know that I have the power of choice.

CHAPTER 10

SECRETS REVEALED

"The device was a gift from a faraway country," the Gentle Hero revealed. "It was meant to bring good things to the City and was received with gratitude from the king. The Guardians have been trained and can use it wisely. They know all about its wonders, but they also know about its potential dangers. They don't want what happened to you to happen to anyone else."

"Ah... so this is why The Guardians go to great lengths to hide the device from us." Shadow Boy had told me that in the beginning.

"Yes," said the Gentle Hero. "The king has ordered this device to only be used by those who are trained to navigate its depths—using it in ways which reflect Guardian values."

Then the Gentle Hero spoke about some of these dangers and mentioned a word I had not heard before: **"Pornography"**. It's an enemy that lurks in the shadows and demands secrecy.

All of a sudden, what I had seen made more sense! "So, pornography is like a murky mess that wants to stay hidden. But talking about my experience brings it out of the shadows where I can make wise choices!"

"You catch on quick!" said the Gentle Hero.

"You know, pornography is not something that The Guardians choose for themselves either. It's part of a world The Guardians reject."

The Gentle Hero helped me to see how pornography was the opposite of what we worked hard to value and protect in ourselves and others. "Rather than respect, some people choose disrespect. Rather than kindness, some people choose to allow violence. Rather than using strength wisely, some people misuse their power."

"Wow! I'm not sure I understand everything yet, but it's starting to make sense."

The Gentle Hero smiled. "I promise you that I will be there to help and train you to better understand the skills that you need to navigate this new world and the devices yet to come as you get older."

"Wow! Thank you! I feel so much better knowing that I have someone to teach me how to guard myself!"

The weight I'd dragged out of the city to the Gentle Hero's home dissolved. With a huge hug, I promised to visit again soon.

CHAPTER 11

GETTING STRONGER

Life has now certainly taken on a new chapter. I feel like I can breathe again.

I reckon I might almost be ready to be a Guardian!

The Gentle Hero continues to share so many wise things and it's hard to remember everything! On one of my visits, I asked the Gentle Hero to help me write a letter to myself in my diary, so that I wouldn't forget!

Dear Hamish,

On the tough days, remember that even though the city walls can't protect you from those images and thoughts, you can make wise choices and learn to take control!

Be kind to yourself! It might take practice, but you can choose to be strong and skilful to win the internal battle you will sometimes feel.

There are lots of wondrous and helpful things to find on tech devices, but there are also lots of harmful things.

It's up to you to be a guardian of your 'self' so you grow up to be strong, respectful and brave—just like The Guardians.

And most of all, you have made a powerful choice—you have chosen not to invite violent or abusive things into your mind that you know will trouble you. You have chosen to guard yourself and build some protective walls of your own.

I know that there will be many more challenging adventures ahead, but I am stronger now and can be courageous.

Ah ha! I guess because I've learned from my experiences, I qualify to be wise now too!

TRAINING TO BE A GUARDIAN

The Guardians believe in having a strong character. Some of their values are:
- Lead by example
- Be strong yet gentle
- Be respectful
- Be courageous
- Be brave
- Use wisdom

Who do I admire and want to be like? Why do I want to be like them?

....
....
....
....
....
....

What other values do I want for my life? Why?

....
....
....
....
....
....
....
....

Who or what can be a "Shadow Boy"? (Hint: a negative or bad influence.)

....
....
....
....
....
....
....

Hamish experienced early warning signs—this is the body's physiological response to feeling unsafe. Read back through the story and try to list all of the early warning signs Hamish had:

....
....
....
....
....
....
....
....
....
....
....
....
....
....
....
....
....

 SAFETY THEME NUMBER 1:

We all have the right to feel safe all of the time.

 SAFETY THEME NUMBER 2:

We can talk to someone about anything no matter what it is.

Hamish kept many Shadow Secrets (unsafe secrets), each one a little bigger than the last, and they made it very hard for Hamish to feel safe because his early warning signs were telling him that he needed to ask for help.

Some people have other types of Shadow Secrets—they can make people feel bad, uncomfortable or unsafe. What could I DO if I am given a Shadow Secret?

....
....
....
....
....
....
....

If I am curious about something, or want to talk about a Shadow Secret, who are my trusted safe people I can speak to? (Sometimes we call these people our safety team.)

....
....

....

....
....

Talk with someone on your safety team and ask them to help you find the number of a kid's helpline to call. This is so that if one of your safety team aren't around or won't listen, you can always have someone up your sleeve to talk to.

Phone number for Kids Helpline:

....

REMEMBER, if the first person you choose to share your Shadow Secret with doesn't listen or know what to do, it's important to keep telling until someone listens and helps you.

After Hamish spoke to the Gentle Hero, how did he feel?

....
....
....
....
....
....

The Gentle Hero promised to teach Hamish about devices. The devices that I use are:

....
....
....
....
....
....

Who do I know who can teach me to use tech devices safely? (Remember, a Gentle Hero or a Guardian can be either gender!)

....
....
....
....
....
....

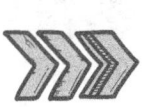 A wise person is someone who learns from their mistakes, respects others and thinks carefully about their choices.

 Learning from what the Gentle Hero shared with Hamish, what parts of 'self' could I be a guardian of?

- Guard the things that go into my M_____

- Be aware of how my B_____ changes

- Keep watch over how my E_____ feel

- Practice self-_____ (tip: it can be tricky to practice this, so ask a trusted adult to help you understand what this means).

By learning to be a guardian of my 'self', I will grow up to be strong, respectful & brave—like The Guardians.

3 STEPS TO BEING SAFE

1. Name the Shadow Secret (whatever that may be).

2. Find a trusted person and share with them.

3. Practice being a guardian of 'self'.

I think being a guardian also means:

....
....
....
....
....

NOTE TO PARENTS, CARERS AND TEACHERS

This book is written to help parents, carers and teachers prepare and assist children to know what to do and how to recover from viewing explicit, harmful and inappropriate content.

Kids are seeing pornography accidentally or deliberately earlier than ever before. In 2008, 14.4% of boys had viewed porn by age 12 or younger. By 2014, this had risen to 48.7%. In 2019, research indicates that 65.5% of boys have seen pornography by age 12 or younger. For girls of the same age, 8.7% had viewed it in 2014, rising to 30% in 2019. Alarmingly, clinicians are reporting cases of children aged as young as five onwards receiving therapeutic interventions.

Developmentally, children have limited experiential and cognitive capacity to understand and interpret what they see. The way that children process pornography varies from child to child; however, reported feelings can range from curiosity, disgust, confusion, guilt and arousal. "I hated this, but I liked it". "I don't want to look at more, but I really want to look at more". "I think it's bad for me, but I don't really know why". Internal conflict without the knowledge of why porn is unhealthy, can quickly lead to children believing unhelpful sexual stories (scripts) about themselves and others, which are embedded in violence and inequality, shame and secrecy—unhealthy foundations for brain development and building positive relationships.

Additionally, there are a growing number of children who see pornography and then act out inappropriate behaviours on other children. This provides an even greater need for all children to have comprehensive protective behaviours education that includes online safety and an awareness of how to respond to pornography.

Hamish and the Shadow Secret is an educational resource for engaging children in a safe and robust conversation about the harms of pornography. Written for children aged 8-12-years, Hamish and the Shadow Secret is a valuable inclusion in every home, school and counselling setting.

FURTHER INFORMATION AND RESOURCES CAN BE FOUND AT www.shadowsecret.info

SCHOOL RESOURCES

Comprehensive educational materials to complement Hamish and the Shadow Secret are available in the "The Guardian" Unit of IQ PROGRAMS.

An initiative of Youth Wellbeing Project under the direction of Liz Walker, IQ PROGRAMS equip educators for tricky conversations – learn more at www.iqprograms.com.

ABOUT THE AUTHOR

Liz Walker is an accredited sexuality educator, speaker and author, dedicated to culture-shifting initiatives that respond to pornography harms on children + young people. Liz holds three distinct yet complementary roles. Schools and community education as Managing Director of Youth Wellbeing Project: providing holistic relationships + sexuality education to prevent sexual harms, enhance children and young people's relationships, and build resilience to porn culture; advocacy as the Deputy Chair of the Australian registered health promotion charity eChildhood: dedicated to mobilizing responses that reduce the harmful effects of pornography on children and young people; and parent education in her role as Director of Health Education at Culture Reframed, the global lead in solving the public health crisis of the digital age.

Well-connected internationally, Liz regularly provides consultancy to government, non-profit, and professional organizations. Educators throughout Australia and internationally utilize the Youth Wellbeing Project IQ PROGRAMS, authored by Liz and her team, underpinned by holistic sexuality education principles. Her work includes the children's book: Not for Kids! which was published in February 2016 for 5-10-year-olds.

Hamish and the Shadow Secret is Liz's second children's book, written for 8-12-year-olds. Both books are a 'must have' for parents and professionals to prepare kids for the inevitable occasion of when they will see explicit imagery.

ABOUT THE CO-AUTHOR AND ILLUSTRATOR

Don Truss is a school chaplain and has been positively impacting kids in this role for 11 years.

He has gained a wealth of experience, having worked to support children and youth in various roles over last 18 years. Don has a passion to see young people succeed and flourish in life, as well as gain necessary tools to navigate current and emerging challenges.

Don has had the pleasure of co-authoring and illustrating *Hamish and the Shadow Secret* with Liz Walker. He hopes this tool will empower kids and equip parents and care givers to support and protect our young people from pornography harms. This invaluable book will create opportunity for open and constructive conversations to address this important child safety issue.

Don is also husband to Miriam and father to four children.

www.ingramcontent.com/pod-product-compliance
Lightning Source LLC
Chambersburg PA
CBHW050607300426
44112CB00013B/2106